Coaching for Development
Skills for Managers and Team Leaders

Marianne Minor, M.S.W.

A Fifty-Minute™ Series Book

This Fifty-Minute™ Book is designed to be "read with a pencil." It is an excellent workbook for self-study as well as classroom learning.

Coaching for Development

Skills for Managers and Team Leaders

Marianne Minor, M.S.W.

CREDITS:

Managing Editor:	**Kathleen Barcos**
Editor:	**Robert Racine**
Typesetting:	**ExecuStaff**
Cover Design:	**Amy Shayne**
Cartoonist:	**Ralph Mapson**

For more information contact:

Course Technology
25 Thomson Place
Boston, MA 02210

Or find us on the Web at **www.courseilt.com**

For permission to use material from this text or product, submit a request online at www.thomsonrights.com.

Trademarks

Disclaimer

ISBN 1-56052-319-0

Printed in the United States of America

1 2 3 4 5 PM 06 05 04 03

Learning Objectives for

Coaching for Development

The learning objectives for *Coaching for Development* are listed below. They have been developed to guide you, the reader, to the core issues covered in this book.

The Objectives of this book are:

❏ 1) To explain the role of manager as coach

❏ 2) To clarify the meaning for five roles of coaches

❏ 3) To give examples of techniques in quality coaching decisions

About the Author:

Marianne Minor is president of her own consulting company, Marianne Minor and Associates in Silicon Valley, California. This company specializes in management, leadership and organizational development. Marianne has over fifteen years experience working both internally and externally in Fortune 500 companies. She has designed core curriculum for Pacific Gas and Electric Co., trained all levels of management at General Electric on leadership skills and consulted with California school districts on decentralized decision making, feedback systems and building teams. In addition, she has taught at the graduate level at San Jose State University and the University of San Francisco. She has a B.A. In Psychology, an M.S.W. and is a Licensed Clinical Social Worker. The author may be contacted through Crisp Publications.

CONTENTS

SECTION

I

The New Role of Manager as Coach

MANAGERS' NEW ROLES

Major changes or trends in the past decade have affected the traditional role of the manager in corporations. Traditional managers have designed and allocated work, set goals, and monitored their realization through a system of measurements and controls. The trend now is for management jobs to be reduced, eliminated or redefined. Managers are encouraged to be facilitators who empower through a common vision, and team leaders who motivate and lead. Confused as to their roles, managers don't even know what to call themselves—team leaders, project leaders, coaches.

Managers must coach using strong interpersonal skills to provide the right advice, support, assignments, and resources at the right time to a large number of individuals and teams.

TEN TRENDS CHANGING MANAGERS' ROLES

#1. Restructuring

Due to intensified worldwide competition, many corporations have been forced to undergo major restructuring that has reduced the levels of management and increased the speed with which organizations can respond to changes in the global marketplace and the needs of the increasingly demanding customer. As organizations go from being hierarchical to lateral, the formal power of managers has diminished and the boundaries between managers and workers has begun to blur. In fact, jobs have become so broad in scope that many workers have managerial responsibilities without the title, and sometimes without the pay.

#2. Temporary Workers

The corporation is becoming a community of temporary workers. Many companies are outsourcing more of their functions to vendors in an attempt to access more specialized skills and control costs. For the manager, it requires developing positive relationships with a large group of temporary employees who may vary in their level of commitment. For the worker with specialized skills, it may mean more financially and professionally rewarding work. It could also mean, however, living in a perpetual state of anxiety about job security.

#3. Globalization

Many companies have realized the business opportunities in Asia and under-developed countries and are moving into these areas with needed products and services. Working with diversity and learning how to do business in different cultures have created many problems. In India for example, some companies have found it difficult to deal with centralized government regulations to do business. Many businesses see tremendous opportunities in Mexico, Malaysia and India as a result of a growing middle class and a demand for more products. Companies will have to learn to deal with different ways of life and cultural norms in conducting business. Managers will have to value diversity in working with indigenous workers, adapt to changes in business practices, and empower people who work in remote field locations.

#4. New Technologies

The development of new technologies may create more efficient organizations and force workers to learn new skills quickly and adapt to change at an increased pace. Faxes, e-mail, pagers, and portable phones make people always available. There is an expectation that employees should be available twenty-four hours a day, seven days a week, and be able to respond to requests quickly from wherever they are. The notion of working anyplace any time is taking hold, with many employees telecommuting and doing extensive travel.

#5. Reengineering

Many companies are trying to use such tools as process mapping and the creative use of information technology to redesign their business process, reduce cycle time as well as bureaucracy, and enhance their productivity.

#6. Ownership

Creating "ownership" at lower levels can have positive and negative consequences on job satisfaction. Many decisions have been decentralized as a result of the delayering process, so workers may have more input into decisions that affect them. Jobs will have broader definitions, and the focus will be on lateral rather than vertical movement. There may not be the opportunities to move up, but engineers and other technical people may have some managerial responsibilities without the titles, pay, or prestige associated with them. They may not be interested in the interpersonal role of being a manager and may resent having to do nontechnical work as part of their jobs. They may not possess the skills to coach.

TEN TRENDS CHANGING MANAGERS' ROLES (continued)

#7. Accelerating Change

The accelerated rate of change will require the development of employee skills. This will require that managers effectively utilize what little time they have with their employees to enhance their skills and confidence in taking on greater levels of responsibility. It will mean training others how to be coaches. Managers will have to be skilled teachers who understand how employees learn best. They will also have to facilitate change and counsel people through the stages of change.

Employees who are resilient may rise to the challenge and be excited by their new roles, but some will resist and continue to talk about "the good old days." Since corporations can no longer offer job security, mobility, or the complete range of benefits they once did, layoffs will become an issue.

Managers will have to be more creative in motivating employees and assigning them exciting work so that employees develop new skills and stay employable in the marketplace. Employees will need to develop an attitude of self-employment and self-reliance wherever they work.

#8. Self-Directed Teams

With a focus on examining and improving business processes and products, people with different skills are working in teams to set goals as well as schedules, and in some cases, selecting, training, coaching, and even terminating workers. Some workers thrive on this level of empowerment and enjoy the additional challenges, but others resent the new level of responsibility.

Organizations are having to revise their compensation systems to establish team rewards in order to motivate employees.

#9. Demographic Shifts

Shifting workforce demographics. The terms "managing diversity" and "valuing diversity" are being taught, from public-sector organizations such as county offices to small and large private companies.

Managing diversity is not the same as affirmative action or equal opportunity employment. The objective is not to assimilate women and minorities into the dominant white male culture, but to create a heterogeneous culture that fosters the full potential of all. Copeland Griggs Productions, Inc., which developed one of the first video-based training programs on diversity, defines "valuing diversity" as "recognizing and appreciating that individuals are different, that diversity is an advantage if it is valued and well managed, that diversity is not to be simply tolerated but encouraged, supported, and nurtured."[1]

While most American corporations have some kind of corporate initiative about managing a diverse workforce, changing people's beliefs, values, and attitudes is not an easy task.

There is a lot of controversy about how to train people in managing or valuing diversity and very little scientific research that demonstrates that training can impact the kinds of beliefs that are created in one's formative years. Yet companies are recognizing that while their workforces are becoming more diverse, so are their customer bases and their stakeholders. Experts agree that managing diversity should be seen as part of a business strategy to stay competitive in an increasingly competitive marketplace.

New demographics are forcing companies to create policies, promotional opportunities, and job descriptions that encourage the use of everyone's unique talents.

Through trial and error, organizations are discovering that managing diversity requires a long-term commitment and a wide variety of programs that impact the culture of the company. By changing their criteria for employee selection, promotion and development opportunities, as well as making the work schedule and environment more flexible, companies may be able to recruit and retain the skilled workers with different backgrounds needed to succeed.

---

[1] Copeland Griggs Productions, Inc. *Personnel Journal.* 1988.

TEN TRENDS CHANGING MANAGERS' ROLES (continued)

#10. Women-Owned and -Managed Businesses

Traditional corporations were created for men by men, and women who wished to move up the ranks have been under social and political pressure to behave "more like a man." Because of this attitude and lack of promotional opportunities, women are leaving large corporations and starting their own companies. Indeed, recent studies show that it is a frustration with career progress, not the call of home and children, that has been driving professional women out of big corporations.[2]

Women-owned businesses employ more people than all of the Fortune 500 companies. The fastest growing sector is small to midsize businesses owned by women. During the 1980s the number of women-owned start-ups grew at twice the rate of all other U.S. business start-ups.

The old management model was of white males using the military approach of control and command. Men who may have learned to work in military hierarchies will have to shift their dominating style to an empowerment and partnership style when working with women.

The new model of management views the organization as a "community," where creativity and compassion are encouraged by a nurturing style of leadership.

Managers will have to understand the positive and negative outcomes of these trends and attempt to address them personally and professionally. How do these trends affect you and your business?

---

[2] "Don't Blame the Baby: Why Women Leave the Corporation." Vicky Tasjian. Wick and Company. 1990.

EXERCISE: The Ten Trends

1. Which of these ten trends are affecting you as an individual the most and why?

_____

_____

2. What will you have to do personally and professionally to cope with this change?

_____

_____

3. Which of these trends are affecting your business the most?

_____

_____

4. What will your business have to do to cope with these changes?

_____

_____

5. How can you prepare your employers to cope with these changes?

_____

_____

6. How can you prepare your employees to cope with these changes?

_____

_____

This book will give you many ideas on how you can capitalize on the positive, and minimize the negative, outcomes of these trends by developing yourself as a skilled and versatile coach.

LONG-TERM IMPLICATIONS

So what are the implications of these trends for managers of the future?

Managers will need to shift:

FROM	TO
Controlling and commanding	Coaching and empowerment
Creating conformity	Valuing diversity
Working through chain of command	Making decision at the lowest levels
Narrow job descriptions	Broad job designs
Leading teams	Teams leading themselves
Developing and rewarding through upward mobility	Developmental assignments and lateral mobility
Domestic focus	Global focus
Using formal power	Using influence
Using imposed systems of measurements and controls	Letting employees determine both
Resisting change	Leading change

The Positive Impact

Hopefully, as a result of these trends, work will become more satisfying as non-value-added work is eliminated or streamlined. Workers will have a greater sense of closure and accomplishment from their jobs as they perform complete tasks and have more control over decisions that affect their jobs. In addition, they will have more power to really affect the business and use their skills.

These trends can have such positive consequences if managers learn how to create a culture of continuous improvement, understand their new roles, develop employees, and coach effectively. In the next section, we define coaching for development and explore the benefits of doing it.

SECTION

II

Coaching for Development

WHAT IS COACHING FOR DEVELOPMENT?

Coaching for development is a process of building a working environment and relationship that enhances the development of skills and the performance of one or both parties. Coaching must be supported and reinforced by the performance management system and the business culture.

What is "development"? It is identifying activities to prepare employees for greater scope or depth in their current or future positions. Effective development should increase the personal growth and job satisfaction of employees.

What's In It for Business?

- Enhances worker productivity and performance

- Increases retention of employees

- Ensures good labor pool because of superior reputation

- Boosts motivation and commitment to corporate values and vision

- Enables employees to respond quickly and more favorably to change

What's In It for Employees?

- Helps employees grow

- Keeps their skills current

- Increases involvement in decision making and managing

- Gives employees greater visibility and exposure to information

What's In It for Team Leaders?

- Supports shared leadership responsibilities

- Gives satisfaction of watching employees grow

- Enhances reputation for developing people

- Provides more opportunities for delegation

- Frees time to pursue visioning, team building and recognizing employees

COACHING LEVELS

There are a variety of approaches a team leader or manager can take in coaching depending on the level of performance of the employee, the manager–employee relationship, and the goal of the coaching session. Three different approaches commonly used are:

(Level One)   *To improve substandard performance*

The manager should use a directive approach to set standards and review expectations if an employee does not know what to do or how to perform a particular task.

(Level Two)   *To maintain standard performance*

The manager or team leader uses a variety of reinforcement and reward strategies to keep employees interested/satisfied enough to come to work, as well as meet most of the demands and standards of the job.

(Level Three)   *Developmental coaching to exceed standard performance and develop new skill sets*

The manager or team leader assesses the employee's development needs and provides customized opportunities both on and off the job to those who are already meeting job expectations.

This will ensure that employees will be continually motivated to take on new tasks and responsibilities. The purpose of level three coaching is to assist the employee in moving to the next level of responsibility in job scope or depth. This may not necessarily mean an upward promotion, since there are less and less levels to advance through in today's organizations. This involves creating a partnership in which the needs of both the organization and the employee are examined.

This book focuses on this third type of coaching from a systems point of view. All coaching must be considered in the context of the larger corporate culture and existing systems, such as for hiring, performance monitoring and evaluation, compensation, and succession, since each organization is vastly different. How employees or managers do their jobs may vary widely across companies. For example, how an employee in Company A runs a meeting may be quite different for someone in Company B. Some cultures are very disciplined about beginning a meeting on time, whereas others are much more casual about beginning a meeting 10 minutes late. A manager at IBM may determine a set of behaviors, skills and values that are essential to an employee's success, but these same behaviors may be considered heresy at a start-up company where job designs are loosely determined and much broader. Therefore it is crucial that the distinct aspects of the corporate culture are taken into account when defining skills, behaviors or competencies to coach.

In Section III we will examine a systems approach to coaching for development. We will have an opportunity to review some best practices and assess what we are currently doing in relation to these best practices.

SECTION

A Systems Approach for Development

THE FIVE PHASES OF DEVELOPMENT

Effective managers must possess a broad view of the business and its environment, as well as an understanding of human behavior in an organizational setting.
They must view the organization as a set of systems that can be used to motivate,
empower and excite employees, or stifle, control and demotivate them. It is ideal if
a manager can use the human resource systems to create a culture that supports
employee development. The following five-phase process offers numerous best
practices for accomplishing this.

A systems approach for development is a dynamic, ongoing, five-phase process
that requires different roles and skills for team leaders in creating a culture of
continuous improvement.

THE FIVE-PHASE PROCESS

PHASE 1: CREATE A CULTURE OF CONTINUOUS
IMPROVEMENT

PHASE 2: FOSTER TEAMWORK

PHASE 3: ANALYZE COMPETENCIES AND ASSESS
DEVELOPMENTAL NEEDS

PHASE 4: PROVIDE DEVELOPMENTAL OPPORTUNITIES
AND SUPPORT

PHASE 5: CONDUCT COACHING SESSIONS FOR SUCCESS

THE FIVE PHASES OF DEVELOPMENT (continued)

PHASE 1: CREATE A CULTURE OF CONTINUOUS IMPROVEMENT

Managers who attempt to conduct coaching sessions without building a solid foundation will find themselves on very shaky ground. Unless you establish a context, a culture of continuous improvement first, coaching sessions will be futile.

EXERCISE: Best Practices Check-Up

Assess your use of these best practices for creating a culture of continuous improvement.

KEY

1—Major development needed   3—Minor development needed
2—Moderate development needed   4—Little or no development needed

Best Practices	Developmental Needs			
► Collects data and gathers feedback from internal and external stakeholders about the quality of the products and services the organization creates and sells.	1	2	3	4
► Acts upon this feedback to develop ongoing improvement plans.	1	2	3	4
► Collects data and information to monitor progress toward the realization of the company vision and goals.	1	2	3	4
► Asks "what if" and "why" questions to help solve old problems with new solutions.	1	2	3	4

► Demonstrates a willingness to make changes based on significant shifts in the business environment in order to improve the quality of the product and services needed for customer satisfaction.   1 2 3 4

► Encourages innovation within the company from the bottom up.   1 2 3 4

► Involves the employees in reviewing progress toward goals and ongoing implementation plans.   1 2 3 4

► Encourages open sharing and broad-based input by employees in decision making and in establishing new directions and goals   1 2 3 4

► Pursues and provides opportunities for risk taking to enhance personal and professional growth.   1 2 3 4

► Encourages experimentation with new technologies, processes, and services to improve business processes and increase efficiency.   1 2 3 4

TOTALS

Scoring:

30–40: Congratulations! You are implementing many of the best practices.

20–29: Good work! Ask your employees which of these you should do more of.

Below 20: Study each of these practices and begin to implement them now!

THE FIVE PHASES OF DEVELOPMENT (continued)

PHASE 2: FOSTER TEAMWORK

Managers must facilitate work within a complex web of networks, alliances, joint ventures, and cross-functional teams of workers, vendors and sometimes even customers. They are expected to lead two to even five teams, domestically and internationally, by using collaborative processes and joint decision making.

EXERCISE: *Teamwork Quick Check*

Assess your use of these best practices to foster teamwork.

KEY

1—Major development needed   3—Minor development needed
2—Moderate development needed   4—Little or no development needed

Best Practices	Developmental Needs
► Communicates the company vision and values so that everyone can see what his or her role and contribution could be.	1 2 3 4
► Schedules and conducts regular meetings to review progress toward goals and helps team members make appropriate adjustments.	1 2 3 4
► Involves individuals, departments and appropriate teams and groups in planning strategies, goals and processes to ensure ownership of plans.	1 2 3 4
► Publishes team successes to the rest of the company.	1 2 3 4

► Celebrates on the completion of major activities or projects with the team regularly. 1 2 3 4

► Gives praise, credit and recognition to all team members. 1 2 3 4

► Encourages the open discussion and exchange of ideas within and across departments and teams. 1 2 3 4

► Encourages attention to group process; supports team review about how well team members interact with each other and other teams and customers. 1 2 3 4

► Utilizes team reward systems whenever possible. 1 2 3 4

► Builds partnerships up, down, across and outside the company to promote business results. 1 2 3 4

TOTALS [ ] [ ] [ ] [ ]

Scoring:

30–40: Congratulations! You are implementing many of the best practices.

20–29: Good work! Ask your employees which of these you should do more of.

Below 20: Study each of these practices and begin to implement them now!

THE FIVE PHASES OF DEVELOPMENT
(continued)

PHASE 3: ANALYZE COMPETENCIES AND ASSESS DEVELOPMENTAL NEEDS

Managers must determine the criteria or standards to be used in assessing employees, as well as their potential for ongoing development. Managers must also examine job descriptions and define the core competencies of each job in their business culture. Then they must determine which employees possess these competencies. A job competency can be defined as a characteristic within a person, such as a motive, trait, skill, set of experiences, or body of knowledge.[4] Employees' competencies can be determined by observing their behavior. Managers must analyze what set of knowledge, skills, and experiences their high-performing employees possess and identify the specific behaviors that support competency. Only when this is completed, can the manager begin to think about options for development. In addition, a manager must observe employees and assess what they can and cannot do.

EXERCISE: Employees' Needs Analysis Review

Assess your use of these best practices for analyzing competencies and assessing development needs.

KEY

1—Major development needed   3—Minor development needed
2—Moderate development needed   4—Little or no development needed

Best Practices	Developmental Needs
▶ Describes the behaviors that would demonstrate the existence of competency. For example, organizing the text of the presentation, assessing the needs of the audience, setting up the room, and knowing how to use visual aids are all elements of giving an effective presentation.	1 2 3 4

[4] Boyatsis, Richard. *The Competent Manager.* John Wiley and Sons. 1982

► Determines the areas of competencies that make up employees' jobs—for example, giving presentations, running meetings interviewing people.

1 2 3 4

► Observes numerous samples of performance in the context of the competencies and compares the observable performance to the behaviors.

1 2 3 4

► Helps employees test the probable reality of career goals.

1 2 3 4

► Probes employees' accomplishments, skills, interests, and values when discussing what areas to focus on.

1 2 3 4

► Encourages employees to share their perceptions of themselves and to assess their strengths and needs.

1 2 3 4

► Reviews their observations and ratings with employees and strives to reach agreement between self- and other-perceptions.

1 2 3 4

► Describes the competencies most important in the culture.

1 2 3 4

► Develops mutual action plans for development, including what each person will do, and sets dates for their accomplishment.

1 2 3 4

► Seeks creative activities for development that are tailored to the needs, goals and experiences of the individual.

1 2 3 4

TOTALS ☐☐☐☐

Scoring:

30–40: Congratulations! You are implementing many of the best practices.

20–29: Good work! Ask your employees which of these you should do more of.

Below 20: Study each of these practices and begin to implement them now!

THE FIVE PHASES OF DEVELOPMENT (continued)

PHASE 4: PROVIDE DEVELOPMENTAL OPPORTUNITIES AND SUPPORT

Managers need to create a partnership with employees for development to occur. They must involve employees in setting goals and determining appropriate activities to develop competencies.

EXERCISE: Planning and Providing Developmental Opportunities

Assess your use of these best practices for creating plans and providing developmental opportunities and support.

KEY

1—Major development needed   3—Minor development needed
2—Moderate development needed   4—Little or no development needed

Best Practices	Developmental Needs			
► Provides training opportunities for team members to develop new skills.	1	2	3	4
► Allows people to learn from their mistakes.	1	2	3	4
► Encourages team members to use their own judgment in making decisions and solving problems in their new assignments.	1	2	3	4
► Provides time and resources for employees to learn new skills and take on new responsibilities.	1	2	3	4

► Seeks alternative methods for development, not just sending employees to training classes. 1 2 3 4

► Builds on employees' strengths by giving assignments related to their areas of interest. 1 2 3 4

► Focuses on a few critical competencies at one time. 1 2 3 4

► Encourages team members to initiate tasks or projects they think are important. 1 2 3 4

► Involves employees in creating a partnership for developing their competencies. 1 2 3 4

► Transfers responsibility for new assignments gradually so that employees do not feel overwhelmed. 1 2 3 4

TOTALS

Scoring:

30–40: Congratulations! You are implementing many of the best practices.

20–29: Good work! Ask your employees which of these you should do more of.

Below 20: Study each of these practices and begin to implement them now!

DEVELOPMENT SHOULD:

✔ **UPGRADE SKILLS**

✔ **BOOST CONFIDENCE**

✔ **ENHANCE KNOWLEDGE**

✔ **PROMOTE WILLINGNESS TO TAKE RISKS**

THE FIVE PHASES OF DEVELOPMENT (continued)

Options for Development

Successful development plans should have the following aspects:

- Limited focus with no more than two or three areas for development
- Joint responsibility for the process of implementation
- A variety of activities for development
- Well-defined areas of skill and knowledge to be developed
- Resources available
- Specific time frames for accomplishment

Check those activities that could be considered developmental for an employee.

☐ **1.** Increased responsibility in scope of current job—working with larger numbers of employees and teams, cross-functional groups and offshore locations

☐ **2.** Working with mergers, acquisitions, or new divisions that are growing to improve business results

☐ **3.** Increased responsibility in depth of current job—coordinating, managing or evaluating the work of others

☐ **4.** Special projects

☐ **5.** Task forces

☐ **6.** Long vacations

☐ **7.** Chairing a committee

☐ **8.** Teaching others

☐ **9.** Job rotation

☐ **10.** Planning events

☐ **11.** Interviewing experts

☐ **12.** Mentoring others

☐ **13.** Coaching others

☐ **14.** Leading continuous improvement teams

☐ **15.** Lateral transfers

☐ **16.** Sabbaticals

☐ **17.** Attending conferences or meetings

☐ **18.** Temporary promotion

☐ **19.** Completing a feedback profile

☐ **20.** Developing a training manual

☐ **21.** Implementing a change in policy or procedure

☐ **22.** Conducting layoffs or a reorganization

☐ **23.** Negotiating for resources at a higher level

☐ **24.** Running meetings

☐ **25.** Giving presentations

☐ **26.** Facilitating conflict resolution between two employees or teams

☐ **27.** Coursework—formal and informal training, internal and external

☐ **28.** Self-development—books, tapes, CD-ROM

All but the long vacation option can be considered developmental, although some people may disagree!

EMPLOYEE DEVELOPMENT GUIDELINES AHEAD

THE FIVE PHASES OF DEVELOPMENT (continued)

Employee Development Guidelines

It is important to follow a single criteria when determining the best development option. Use the following guidelines to choose the best option:

- ► Tailor the options to the individual's short- and long-term goals.

- ► Analyze which competencies are most critical for the current job and build those first. Then consider those needed for the next assignment.

- ► Assess the resources available: How much will it cost? How long will it take? How much time off the job is needed?

- ► Compared with other employees' skills and potential in the unit, should the resources be spent on this employee? What will be the return on investment?

- ► Determine which competencies are most critical to the business now.

- ► Choose no more than two or three areas for development in order to stay focused.

- ► Try to build on the employee's strengths.

- ► Attempt to match the needs of the individual to the needs of the business whenever possible.

All employees should reflect on their careers at least once a year and take steps to assume responsibility for their future direction. They need to review their job performance and determine their strengths and developmental needs. Most employees need support in doing this, so a manager should facilitate this process by requesting that the employee think through and complete a self-assessment before a coaching discussion can occur.

To assist with this process, consider using the following forms. Have employees complete the career planning self-assessment form before scheduling the coaching session so that your time is well spent.

Career Planning Self-Assessment Form

What are my strengths in my current position?

1. _____

2. _____

3. _____

What are my developmental needs in my current position?

1. _____

2. _____

3. _____

What developmental activities would be most useful to me now?

1. _____

2. _____

3. _____

What is my desired next job assignment?

_____

_____

What competencies will I need to build to be ready for this assignment?

_____

_____

What developmental activities would be most helpful to me in building these?

_____

_____

THE FIVE PHASES OF DEVELOPMENT (continued)

As the manager, you may wish to use the following worksheet to help you prepare for the sessions.

Manager's Worksheet for Developmental Planning

Employee Name: _____

What are the employee's strengths in the current job?

1. _____
2. _____
3. _____
4. _____

What necessary competencies in the employee's current job need development?

1. _____
2. _____
3. _____
4. _____

What competencies are needed for the employee's future assignment?

1. _____
2. _____
3. _____
4. _____

MANAGER'S WORKSHEET (continued)

List desired learning activities according to priority:

High priority: _____

Medium priority: _____

Low priority: _____

List learning activities chronologically:

   1. _____

   2. _____

   3. _____

   4. _____

List and date actions the employee will take:

   1. _____

   2. _____

   3. _____

   4. _____

List and date actions the manager will take:

   1. _____

   2. _____

   3. _____

   4. _____

If a manager has determined that training, either on or off the job, is the best option, then it is crucial that the money and time spent on training are maximized. Review the following guidelines to ensure a return on your investment.

THE FIVE PHASES OF DEVELOPMENT (continued)

Ten Ways to Turn Training into Performance

Check those that you have used to maximize the impact of training.

☐ 1. Determine how the content and methods of the course will build core competencies related to current or future job performance.

☐ 2. Match the training to the development needs.

☐ 3. Involve the employee in choosing the course.

☐ 4. Schedule the employees' work so that they can get away from their jobs for the duration of training.

☐ 5. Send employees for training at the right time—right before they will need to use their new knowledge and skills on the job.

☐ 6. Encourage employees to share their new knowledge. Ask them to give presentations to their teams about what was most useful from the course.

☐ 7. Conduct pre-course goal-setting sessions and post-course reviews about what was learned and how it can be applied.

☐ 8. Observe the employees using the new skills and give reinforcement.

☐ 9. Remove barriers to using the new skills.

☐ 10. Model the skills that employees have learned.

PHASE 5: CONDUCT COACHING SESSIONS FOR SUCCESS

Finally, if managers have built a solid foundation for the corporate culture, established their credibility and a relationship of trust, then they can begin phase 5, which is face-to-face coaching.

EXERCISE: Coaching Checkpoint

Assess your use of these best practices for conducting coaching sessions:

KEY

1—Major development needed   3—Minor development needed
2—Moderate development needed   4—Little or no development needed

Best Practices	Developmental Needs
► Encourages the open airing of problems as well as differences of opinion and seeks a positive resolution.	1 2 3 4
► Develops contracts with employees around observing and evaluating performance.	1 2 3 4
► Provides specific, timely feedback to team members, both positive and corrective.	1 2 3 4
► Encourages team members to find and correct their own errors, rather than delegating this task upward.	1 2 3 4
► Invites employees to assess their competencies and join in the search for development plans.	1 2 3 4

THE FIVE PHASES OF DEVELOPMENT (continued)

Best Practices	Developmental Needs			
▶ Addresses performance problems in a direct, constructive way.	1	2	3	4
▶ Holds employees accountable for meeting their commitments.	1	2	3	4
▶ Builds self-esteem by attacking problems, not people.	1	2	3	4
▶ Discusses what employees have learned and how current skills can be enhanced with new assignments.	1	2	3	4
▶ Gets agreement on standards for performance of new tasks and monitors and supports high performance.	1	2	3	4
TOTALS				

Scoring:

30–40: Congratulations! You are implementing many of the best practices.

20–29: Good work! Ask your employees which of these you should do more of.

Below 20: Study each of these practices and begin to implement them now!

After a manager has built the foundation, he or she can begin to explore the best approach to take with each employee during the coaching process.

SECTION

IV

The Roles of a Coach

THE FIVE ROLES OF A COACH

Most employees need to have a clear understanding of their roles in an organization to be effective in their jobs. Certain questions are foremost in their minds as they learn how to do their jobs in a particular corporate culture.

> The job of a coach is to hear these questions and assist the employee in answering them.

Major Questions Employees Want Answered

► How am I doing?

► How do others see me?

► What is expected of me?

► How can I best perform my current job?

► What is this corporate culture like?

► How can I get where I want to go from here?

► Can I take risks here?

► Am I being paid to think or just execute?

► What are the rewards for working hard?

► How can you, as my manager, help me realize current job satisfaction and long-term career goals?

To answer these questions, a manager will need to develop skill in implementing a variety of coaching interventions, which may vary depending on the stage of the process, the employee's development needs, and the goal of the coaching.

THE FIVE ROLES OF A COACH (continued)

There are five different coaching roles appropriate to implementing this process. They are represented by the acronym SMART:

SPONSOR

MENTOR

APPRAISER

ROLE MODEL

TEACHER

These five roles can be assumed by an individual with a formal position of power, such as a manager, or by someone with informal power, such as a team member, as long as it is someone the employees trust and respect. Let's examine these roles in some depth.

 **SPONSOR**

A sponsor gives the high-performing employee exposure to important information, decision makers and other people in the organization, as well as public recognition. The sponsor assists employees in determining assignments that will help them grow and meet their career goals. This role should be used when an employee has demonstrated outstanding skills and contributions and is looking for new challenges to grow.

Best Behaviors for Sponsors

Place a check next to each behavior that you now demonstrate. After reading this book and practicing the exercises, you should be able to confidently place checks next to all of these behaviors.

☐ 1. Seeks and creates opportunities to develop their employees.

☐ 2. Advocates for employees by marketing their skills outside their area of responsibility.

☐ 3. Provides important backing and support to help employees take risks with their careers.

☐ 4. Conducts meaningful career discussions based on the employees' goals, values, skills and interests.

☐ 5. Is willing to share the credit and spotlight to promote employees' interests.

☐ 6. Diagnoses development needs and creates development plans that match.

☐ 7. Exposes employees to social networks inside and outside the organization to broaden their perspectives on field and career options.

☐ 8. Provides information to employees about positions within the organization that are consistent with their goals and about what they can do to advance in the company.

☐ 9. Encourages employees to redesign their jobs around their own capabilities and aspirations.

☐ 10. Creates linkages between current job responsibilities and the development of new competencies.

SPONSOR (continued)

For a sponsor's discussion to be successful, he or she must obtain valuable information from employees in order to plan how they can develop. Review the following questions that a sponsor should ask to obtain this information.

Questions a Sponsor Needs to Ask

Questions to ask employees during a sponsoring session:

► What in your job satisfies or dissatisfies you?

► What are the values you regard as most important in your work?

► What are your major accomplishments? Which of these are you the most proud of? Why?

► What are your areas of interest? What tasks do you find most motivating?

► What skills do you have but have been unable to use on your current job?

► What are your developmental needs? Which needs would you most like to work on now?

► What are your short- and long-term career goals?

► What training classes and on-the-job assignments would be most helpful in fulfilling your developmental needs at this time?

► What people do you need access to? How can I help make the referrals?

► What can I do to support your career growth and job satisfaction?

KEY STEPS FOR SPONSORING SESSIONS

Managers need to have the organizational framework for understanding the role of sponsor, but they also need to have a structure for conducting a sponsoring session. They must know, plan and practice the following steps.

Step 1   **Put the employee at ease** and agree on the purpose of the meeting.

Step 2   **Ask the employee to discuss his or her thoughts** about short- and long-term career goals.

Step 3   **Probe for skills, values, interests, and accomplishments,** using the preceding questions as guidelines. Show interest through effective listening.

Step 4   **Provide information** to the employee about what opportunities exist in current or possible future jobs within the company that relate to his or her career goals.

Step 5   **Explore what assignments, projects or training classes** might be appropriate to work toward the fulfillment of career goals.

Step 6   **Get agreement on the next steps** each of you will take and set a follow-up date.

SPONSOR (continued)

More Tips on Sponsoring

- Keep employees focused on the next career step, which may develop from a greater proficiency, achievement or satisfaction in their current positions, rather than from the elusive promise of mobility in the distant and unpredictable future.

- Find ways to offer a large number of on-the-job developmental opportunities, rather than relying on traditional training. Recent research has shown the value of on-the-job experience and tough assignments over traditional training as critical learning experiences.

- Carefully analyze the training programs available and be sure they provide practical information that will enhance job performance, mesh with the career goals of the employee, and provide chances to practice and get feedback during the training.

- Discuss with employees ahead of time what learning goals they have in relationship to the training and conduct coaching sessions afterward to help them apply what they have learned.

- Make sure the discussion is translated into specific actions each of you will take and that the plan is realistic and can be implemented.

- Help employees take responsibility for their career planning by holding them accountable for their part in the process.

A mentor is one who is involved in a life-long process of self-development, stays current in his or her respective fields, and understands how networks operate. Mentors know how to deal with corporate politics and how to build power through the use of influence. A mentor can help an employee prioritize projects to be done, in terms of the current organizational realities and politics, and provide a set of "best practices" for how to approach a given problem. A mentor can also help an employee understand how change occurs, as well as how to plan for and implement change. A mentor can assist the employee in breaking down barriers to performance and learning how to work within the bureaucracy.

Best Behaviors for Mentors

Place a check next to each behavior that you now demonstrate.

☐ 1. Protects employees from unnecessary stress.

☐ 2. Helps employees avoid getting caught up in no-win political situations that could harm their careers.

☐ 3. Has an open door policy and is accessible to employees.

☐ 4. Shows appreciation for a diversity of opinions, work styles, etc.

☐ 5. Shows employees how to streamline bureaucracy and reduce administrative aspects of the job.

☐ 6. Keeps employees informed on the subtle things going on in the company that may affect their jobs, including norms about dress, leadership styles and how to resolve conflicts.

☐ 7. Maintains confidentiality.

☐ 8. Conveys empathy and support when employees need it.

☐ 9. Assists employees in removing obstacles that may be hindering their development.

☐ 10. Communicates ongoing information about organizational changes and decisions that may affect employees' work and career opportunities.

MENTOR (continued)

Questions a Mentor Needs to Ask

To conduct meaningful mentoring sessions, a manager must be prepared to ask the right questions. Review the following questions that a mentor should ask.

Questions to ask during a mentoring session:

▶ How are you feeling about your current assignment?

▶ What barriers are you experiencing to doing your job effectively?

▶ What can you do to break through these barriers?

▶ What political situations are you encountering that may be causing you difficulty?

▶ What bureaucratic systems seem to be getting in your way and how can you streamline these?

▶ What relationships do you find most or least satisfying?

▶ How can you build better relationships?

▶ What does the ideal organization look like? How can you help create it?

▶ What resources would help you enhance your current and future performance?

▶ How can I help?

FOR KEY STEPS FOR MENTORING, READ ON . . .

KEY STEPS FOR MENTORING SESSIONS

For the discussion to be meaningful, mentors must plan for their sessions and have a structure. Plan the structure of your sessions around the following key steps.

Step 1   **Show interest in employees** by asking questions such as the preceding ones.

Step 2   **Ask employees about barriers** to the performance or development of their desired competencies.

Step 3   **Listen to employees' responses.**

Step 4   **Explore options for removing barriers** and enhancing performance and/or job satisfaction.

Step 5   **Discuss realities of the corporate culture,** politics, personalities or norms that may be applicable.

Step 6   **Encourage employees** to choose the best option for themselves in relationship to their career goals.

Step 7   **Ask how you can provide support,** and end on an encouraging note.

Step 8   **Set a date for a follow-up session.**

An appraiser helps employees assess their strengths, as well as their development needs, blind spots, interests and career goals. The appraiser contracts with the employee to observe his or her performance under certain conditions and provide appropriate feedback and support.

Best Behaviors for Appraisers

Place a check next to each behavior that you now demonstrate.

☐ 1. Analyzes the competencies needed for an employee's current and future responsibilities.

☐ 2. Observes numerous situations where the employee could demonstrate these competencies.

☐ 3. Provides frequent constructive, positive and corrective feedback that focuses on specific, concrete, observable behaviors or competencies.

☐ 4. Addresses performance problems in a direct, constructive way.

☐ 5. Helps employees define performance criteria they can use to judge their own performance.

☐ 6. At evaluation time, compares employees' performance with previously agreed-upon goals and expectations.

☐ 7. Helps employees analyze the reasons for their successes and failures.

☐ 8. Provides appropriate recognition and rewards to employees for results they have achieved on the job.

☐ 9. Makes sure that rewards are commensurate with results and that employees see the relationship between what they do and the recognition they receive.

☐ 10. Encourages employees to get feedback on their performance from the actual users of their work—customers or other team members.

Questions an Appraiser Needs to Ask

You must first build a contract with the employee before holding appraiser sessions. Getting the answers to the following questions will enable you to build that contract.

► What are the competencies that you think are most important for your current job?

► Which of these do you think you currently possess? Which need the most work?

► What do you think are the competencies that are most important for your desired assignments?

► Which of these do you think you currently possess? Which need the most work?

► In what situations within your current job can you demonstrate these competencies?

► In which of these situations can you be observed to demonstrate these competencies?

► Where and when should these observations occur?

► Who should do the observing and provide the feedback?

► Should there be any outside sources of feedback, for example, from customers or vendors?

► How and when would you like the feedback delivered? Do you want positive, negative or mixed feedback and should it be during or after the observation sessions?

APPRAISER (continued)

KEY STEPS FOR APPRAISER SESSIONS

Appraisers must be prepared for these sessions and structure them around certain outcomes. The following steps are recommended for the structure.

Step 1   **Put the employee at ease** and agree on the purpose of the meeting.

Step 2   **Review the reason for the discussion** and the terms of the feedback contract.

Step 3   **Have the employee assess his or her competencies** and behaviors demonstrated during the last observation.

Step 4   **Give your opinion** about the demonstrated competencies and behaviors, focusing on their strengths.

Step 5   **Provide feedback from others,** if previously agreed upon.

Step 6   **Listen to the employee's reaction.**

Step 7   **Ask employees** what methods they could use to enhance the behaviors and build new competencies.

Step 8   **Build on their ideas** whenever possible, and add your own.

Step 9   **Get agreement** on the next steps and set a follow-up date.

ROLE MODEL

Serving as a role model is crucial to coaching, as you have to be seen as trust-worthy, competent and credible in order to coach others. Role models "walk the talk" and demonstrate the appropriate leadership style in their corporate culture.

Best Behaviors for Role Models

Please place a check next to each behavior that you now demonstrate.

☐ 1. Demonstrates enthusiasm for the vision and values of the company.

☐ 2. Pursues opportunities for personal and professional growth.

☐ 3. Stays current in one's field of expertise by reading, attending conferences and networking.

☐ 4. Communicates the reasons behind important changes that are made.

☐ 5. Gives employees the opportunity to voice concerns before changes that are going to affect them are carried out.

☐ 6. Communicates and models the importance of cooperation and collaboration when solving problems and making decisions.

☐ 7. Demonstrates integrity in all dealings with employees and customers alike.

☐ 8. Shows strong interpersonal skills in dealing with employees at all levels.

☐ 9. Builds teams up, down and across through collaborative behavior.

☐ 10. Admits mistakes and grows from them—models continuous improvement philosophy.

There are no questions or key steps for being a role model, since it is the way a manager behaves in everyday life and does not require formal sessions. However, a good coach will search for opportunities to intentionally model certain desirable behaviors relevant to the corporate culture he or she wants to create or support.

54

The role of teacher is important in providing information about a business's strategy, vision, values, services and products, and customers so employees can perform effectively in their jobs.

Employees sometimes need a view of the big picture as well as specific job skills. The teacher provides this, frequently when the business strategy, services or products change, or to orient new employees to the business or introduce a team to a new manager's approach and vision. Teachers also assist employees in learning new job skills, such as budgeting and giving sales presentations.

Best Behaviors for Teachers

Place a check next to each behavior that you now demonstrate.

☐ **1.** Empowers employees by building knowledge and skills for the benefit of both the employee and the organization.

☐ **2.** Demonstrates good written and oral communication skills.

☐ **3.** Shows awareness of different learning styles.

☐ **4.** Objectively observes others and analyzes root causes of positive and negative performance.

☐ **5.** Demonstrates support for employees when they are learning new tasks and roles.

☐ **6.** Provides clarity around performance expectations.

☐ **7.** Lets employees know how they can perform their jobs better.

☐ **8.** Breaks tasks and activities into small meaningful chunks and manageable steps.

☐ **9.** Provides information about general trends in the industry and benchmarking data to use for comparisons.

☐ **10.** Offers technical advice and expertise when needed.

Questions a Teacher Needs to Ask

Managers need to know a great deal about an employee before they begin the teaching process. This information can be obtained by asking the following questions:

► What does the employee know about the company's vision, mission and values?

► What does the employee know about the company's products, services, customers and competitors?

► What do employees think their jobs are?

► Why are their jobs important? How are their jobs linked to the big picture—the end product and end user?

► How do their jobs relate to the work of others?

► What are the standards for their jobs? Why?

► What tasks are they most or least comfortable with?

► Can they best learn their jobs by reading manuals, watching others, attending a class, or trying on their own?

► How fast do they want to learn all the different parts of their jobs?

► How can you help enhance and accelerate their learning process?

Once a manager obtains this information, he or she can use it to determine what style of teaching to use with each employee. Some employees will be more comfortable with formal training sessions; others like more of a "buddy system." A manager should provide employees with all the information they need to build knowledge and skills, but do this without overwhelming them with massive amounts of information they cannot process.

TEACHER (continued)

KEY STEPS FOR TEACHING SESSIONS

When planning for a teaching session, it is ideal to stay focused by following a structure. Use the following steps to stay focused.

Step 1   **Describe why learning the task or procedure is important** to the company, team or individual.

Step 2   **Break the task or procedure into small chunks or** steps.

Step 3   **Verbally explain** how to perform each step of the task or procedure.

Step 4   **When possible, show how** the task or procedure should be performed (this links back to being a role model).

Step 5   **Ask employees to practice** or demonstrate the task or procedure in front of you.

Step 6   **Provide positive feedback** when possible and make specific corrections by giving detailed recommendations on how to do each step more effectively.

Step 7   **Have employees practice again** and provide them with reinforcement.

Step 8   **Ask employees to tell you** when and how they can use the new skill.

Step 9   **Ask employees how you can provide ongoing support** in using the new skill.

EXERCISE: *Describe Best Behaviors*

Describe the behaviors of the best coaches you have known to use these five roles and the impact their behavior had on your performance.

Best Sponsor Behaviors: _____

_____

Impact on Performance: _____

_____

Best Mentor Behaviors: _____

_____

Impact on Performance: _____

_____

Best Appraiser Behaviors: _____

_____

Impact on Performance: _____

_____

Best Role Model Behaviors: _____

_____

Impact on Performance: _____

_____

Best Teacher Behaviors: _____

_____

Impact on Performance: _____

_____

CASE STUDIES: COACHING FOR DEVELOPMENT

Sometimes a manager will use all five coaching roles with one employee. Consider an example from the legal field. An experienced courtroom attorney is responsible for managing new attorneys just out of law school who will be trying criminal cases. He will have to observe the skills of each new attorney and then teach them so they will have a strong knowledge base about the evidence code. Then he will need to be a role model and demonstrate how to select a jury and develop a strategy, discussing the reasons he is doing certain things. He will need to observe their performance and appraise their competencies. He will need to offer suggestions and examples of how to be better prepared for the future. He will need to act as a mentor in helping them adjust their style to a variety of judges. After their competencies are developed on the easier cases, the new attorneys will be assigned tougher and tougher cases. They will increase their knowledge and skill by on-the-job assignments and effective coaching. Their learning curve and hence their productivity can be accelerated by the coaching process. There are numerous daily situations in all kinds of organizations where a coaching role is needed. Use the following situations to apply what you have learned thus far about coaching.

PUT YOUR KNOWLEDGE TO THE TEST

In these situations you will find an employee in need of coaching assistance. Choose one or more of the five roles that best fit each situation: sponsor, mentor, appraiser, role model, teacher. The answers are on page 75 in the back of the book.

1. Shannon, a new accountant in your finance group, has been slow to catch on to the new formatting of the expense reports and budgeting requirements, and you have not had time to orient her to these procedures.

The best role is _____

2. Tony, your production control coordinator, has to coordinate his efforts with those of a co-worker from another area. He is having a tough time getting the information he needs to do his job. He comes to you for advice.

The best role is _____

3. Mary, a sales manager, has shown tremendous initiative and skill in training her employees and getting new accounts. There is a big sales meeting in Hawaii to celebrate the unit's success and to plan for next year. There is an opportunity for a few key people to speak at the meeting and you know Mary has wanted to get some additional visibility.

The best role is _____

4. You administer a department of five secretaries, and one of your most productive nonexempts, Tim, has just completed a bachelor's degree in business in the evening at a local college. There is a big employee ownership project coming up for which he could apply his new skills and knowledge.

The best role is _____

5. Your new regional sales manager, Lee, will be traveling to Hong Kong to meet with a potential new customer. It is important that the meeting go well. Lee is new to the Pacific Rim area and not familiar with the customs. You need to be in Japan the next week and could stop for a few days in Hong Kong.

The best role is _____

PUT YOUR KNOWLEDGE TO THE TEST
(continued)

6. You are the project leader for a group of engineers who work on international projects for six months at a time, building power plants. You know the engineers are very independent and have not had any feedback during the project. You have to make some decisions about which team members should be put on what project next.

The best role is _____

7. You have hired a technical writer, Sandy, who is a wonderful writer but has never been exposed to the specifics of your product lines. Her job will be to write about the products in lay terms so customers can easily use the products.

The best role is _____

8. You are the vice-president of human resources. You have assigned one of your more promising HR representatives to the vice-president of finance, the toughest, most demanding vice-president in the company. The HR representative's job will be to coach this VP and help him build a team in his area.

The best role is _____

9. Avery has been a manager for ten years in Minnesota, where he has proven his skill in building both a solid business and good working relationships with peers, subordinates and management. You have relocated him to California and notice that he is beginning to have problems. His employees are complaining to you about his rigid style of management and feel that he is intolerant of differences between people. He has confessed to you that he finds the California culture quite different and thinks that there is not enough of a work ethic among his people, who are always asking for flexible time and a chance to work at home.

The best role is _____

10. You are in charge of technical training and have been working with Sally, a technical trainer, for five years. Sally was so good at presenting complex data in a simple way that you had her design and deliver a training program for your most important customer. Initially Sally did a good job of implementing the program. She did the same program every week for the last six months. Recently, you have noticed that the evaluations are going down and a number of people have complained about the training being unfocused. Sally appears to come late and leave early.

The best role is _____

11. You have promoted and relocated a high-potential black female to a middle manager job in your manufacturing firm. She was an exceptional first-line manager on the East Coast and was able to build teams and meet tough schedules consistently. She has relocated to your plant in Alabama and is the first black female there in both manufacturing and management. After two months, you notice she is not being included in important lunches, is not informed about important meetings, and is not involved in key decisions by the other managers.

The best role is _____

12. You are the manager in charge of research and development in a manu-facturing company. You have noticed that your engineers are running very ineffective meetings. There does not seem to be an agenda or planning before the meeting, little control during the meeting, and minimal follow-up. As a result, time is being wasted and people are growing frustrated with attending.

The best role is _____

S E C T I O N

V

Tools for Coaches

SIX TOOLS FOR COACHES

Coaching is a way to discover and encourage the potential of employees. It involves a continuous flow of instruction, demonstration, dialog, practice, support, and feedback. It requires creating a partnership based on mutual respect and trust. It requires that managers continually build their skills and polish their tools.

Effective coaching requires knowing when and how to use six key tools.

LISTENING

A coach must physically attend to the employee by minimizing distractions, using eye contact, and demonstrating an open body posture. One way to demonstrate listening is to paraphrase what employees say and show empathy for what they might be feeling. Another way is to ask open-ended questions to show interest and probe for important information. Pay attention to their body posture and other nonverbal signals. Summarize at the end of each discussion.

OBSERVING

Coaches must be skilled in looking and listening, watching and waiting for cues that their employees need help or can take more responsibility and autonomy. They must watch for changes in performance. They should observe employees in a wide variety of situations and see how they react to stress. They must look for opportunities to expand competencies, reinforce effective performance and remove barriers.

ANALYZING

Coaches must know how to determine the root cause if there is a downward trend or change in performance. Is the problem caused by personal issues, a skill deficit or a lack of motivation? Has the employee been doing the job too long? Is the work highly repetitive? Coaches also must be able to assess what causes upward trends so they can be aware of the employee's learning style and what types of reinforcement tend to motivate each person.

SIX TOOLS FOR COACHES (continued)

INTERVIEWING

A coach must be able to formulate useful questions to probe for the employee's skills, values, interests and accomplishments. Coaches must know how to get important information in a way that does not make the employee feel interrogated or defensive.

Open-ended questions encourage employee reflection—for example, How are you feeling about your current job? **Closed-ended** questions probe for specifics—for example, When do you hope to attend that class? **Reflective** questions clarify and ensure understanding—for example, Are you saying you're not sure you want that promotion?

CONTRACTING

Coaching involves creating a partnership, and encouraging employees to take responsibility for their careers. As a result, both parties must build a contract around the expectations and commitments of who will do what. Questions that must be answered include: Who will do what? When? How? What responsibility and authority does each party have? What information will be reported back? When will review meetings take place?

GIVING FEEDBACK

Feedback can dramatically improve the performance of an employee. When giving corrective feedback, coaches must focus on specific observable behaviors, describe what was witnessed, rather than judging it. In addition, the desired behavior must be stated and understood. Simply identifying the negative behavior is not enough. Giving recommendations or suggestions for future behavior can reduce the likelihood of defensive behavior from the employees and leave them with some new approaches to try out.

Coaches must tailor the feedback to the skill and knowledge level of employees receiving it and must be careful not to overload them with too much negative feedback. It is important to preserve self-esteem by concentrating on only two or three areas for change even if there are numerous areas for improvement. Remember to watch for positive behaviors and to praise frequently. For more specific tips, see the following chart that describe four types of feedback and the consequences of each. Then review the examples that are given on how to give effective feedback.

Providing Effective Feedback

Whether you recognize it or not, you are constantly giving feedback. How you provide that feedback will often spell the difference between success or failure.

TYPES OF FEEDBACK

TYPE	DEFINITION	PURPOSE	IMPACT
SILENCE	• No response provided	• Maintain status quo	• Decreases confidence • Reduces performance • Produces paranoia • Creates surprises during performance appraisals
CRITICISM (negative)	• Identifies undesirable behaviors	• Stops undesirable behaviors	• Generates excuses/blaming • Decreases confidence • Leads to avoidance or escape • Can eliminate related behaviors • Hurts relationships
ADVICE	• Identifies results or behaviors desired and specifies how to incorporate them	• Shape or change behaviors or results to increase performance	• Improves confidence • Strengthens relationships • Increases performance
REINFORCEMENT (positive)	• Identifies results or behaviors that were desired, up to or exceeding standards	• Increase desired performance or results	• Boosts confidence • Heightens self-esteem • Increases performance • Enhances motivation

HOW TO GIVE EFFECTIVE FEEDBACK

1. Be *specific* when referring to behavior.

   Bad: "Henry, you are lazy and have a poor attitude toward your job."

   Good: "Henry, you have been 15 minutes late for the last three mornings. Please explain why."

2. Consider your timing. Before the event, give feedback in the form of advice; immediately after the event, give positive feedback.

   Bad: (criticism) "Sally, because you've done such a poor job in the past, I need to preview the speech you plan on giving next week."

   Good: (advice) "Sally, I'd like to review the content of your presentation before your speech next week so you can really do a good job in front of the group."

   Bad: (positive but not specific) "Sally, good speech last week. Keep up the good work!"

   Good: (positive) "Sally, you did an outstanding job in organizing your presentation for the meeting. The speech was well researched and logical."

3. Consider the needs of the person receiving the feedback as well as your own. Ask yourself what he or she will get out of the information. Are you "dumping" or genuinely attempting to improve performance or the relationship?

   Bad: "Sue, you always need help with the newsletter. It's not my responsibility. Don't you think it's about time you learned how to edit the newsletter?"

   Good: "Sue, I know how important it is to you to get the newsletter just right, and I recognize that you're under a lot of pressure right now. I will help you edit it this time, but I want you to take that editing class so you can handle it solo in the future."

4. **Focus on behavior the receiver can do something about.**

   Bad: "Sam, why are you so introverted that you don't like to talk to other people?"

   Good: "Sam, we would appreciate your keeping the team informed about the status of the project."

5. **Avoid labels and judgments by describing rather than evaluating behavior.**

   Bad: "Steve, you are very lazy about improving your skills and don't seem to care about your career here."

   Good: "Steve, I have given you five chances to attend training programs in the last year and you haven't enrolled yet. Is there a problem?"

6. **Define the impact on you, the unit, the team and the company.**

   Bad: "Sarah, can't you ever get your reports to me on time?"

   Good: "Sarah, when you don't get your report to me on time, I can't get my report to my boss on time. This slows up decisions about how resources are allocated to our team for the next month and how fast our company can service our customers."

7. **Use "I" statements as opposed to "You" statements to reduce defensiveness.**

   Bad: "Tim, you are so inconsiderate of other people when you leave your radio on."

   Good: "Tim, when you play your radio in the work area, I lose my concentration. Would you mind turning it off during regular work hours?"

HOW TO GIVE EFFECTIVE FEEDBACK (continued)

8. **Check to be sure your message has been clearly received.**

   Bad: "Mary, I'm sure you got it all, huh?"

   Good: "Mary, do you know what information I need you to record for all my phone messages? Can you explain it to me so I know you understand?

9. **Give the feedback in calm, unemotional words, tone, and body language.**

   Bad: "Joe, you blew it again! Isn't it about time you improved your production with this machine?"

   Good: "Joe, I think there might be some ways you can improve your production with this machine."

Feedback Pointers

➤ *Reinforcement* **is the most effective form of feedback.**

➤ *Criticism* **is the most ineffective form of feedback.**

➤ **The difference between criticism and advice is a difference in** *timing*. **Most criticism can be given as advice.**

➤ **When feedback is mixed, the impact is diluted. The employee becomes confused and doesn't know what to do.**

➤ **Criticism overpowers all other feedback.**

➤ **Silence is not always "golden." It can be interpreted in a variety of ways.**

ACTION PLAN FOR SUCCESS

Now is the time to pull together everything you have learned and create an action plan for coaching for development. Answer each of the following questions to help you put your new knowledge into practice.

1. Describe how you will create a culture of continuous improvement.

   _____

   _____

   _____

2. Describe how you will foster teamwork.

   _____

   _____

   _____

3. Describe how you will analyze competencies that determine success and assess the development needs of employees in relation to these competencies.

   _____

   _____

   _____

4. Describe how you will provide developmental opportunities and support.

   _____

   _____

   _____

5. Describe how you will conduct coaching discussions using the five roles of a coach.

   _____

   _____

   _____

ACTION PLAN FOR SUCCESS (continued)

6. Analyze how you can polish your tools. How will you work on improving the following skills?

  • Listening _____

  • Observing _____

  • Analyzing _____

  • Interviewing _____

  • Contracting _____

  • Giving feedback _____

7. What is your timetable for making these improvements?

  _____

  _____

  _____

8. What barriers will you face as you attempt to implement your plan?

  _____

  _____

  _____

9. How can you break through these barriers?

  _____

  _____

  _____

10. How will you reward yourself for having implemented your plan?

  _____

  _____

  _____

Answers

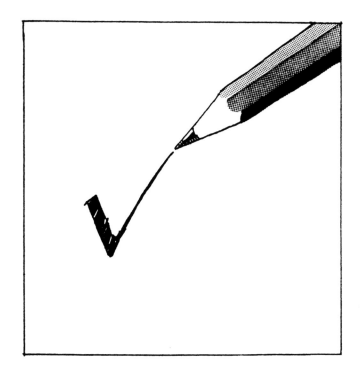

ANSWERS (pages 59–61)

The answers to the case studies are:

1. Teacher

2. Mentor

3. Sponsor

4. Sponsor

5. Role model and Mentor

6. Appraiser

7. Teacher

8. Mentor

9. Mentor

10. Appraiser and Sponsor if the reason for the performance gap is Sally's boredom with her current job. Create a more challenging job design for Sally that has less monotony.

11. Mentor

12. Role Model and Teacher